SHAKER INVENTIONS

SHAKER
INVENTIONS

Nancy O'Keefe Bolick
and
Sallie G. Randoloph

Illustrated by
Melissa Francisco

WALKER AND COMPANY
NEW YORK, NEW YORK

First published in the United States of America by the Walker Publishing Company, Inc.

Published simultaneously in Canada by Thomas Allen and Son, Canada, Limited, Markham, Ontario.

Printed in the United States of America

2 4 6 8 10 9 7 5 3 1

Library of Congress Cataloging-in-Publication Data
Bolick, Nancy O'Keefe.
Shaker Inventions/by Nancy O'Keefe Bolick and Sallie G. Randolph

Includes index.
Summary: Describes the culture and daily way of life of the Shakers and the religious motifs inspiring them.
ISBN 0-8027-6933-0. – ISBN 0-8027-6934-9 (Lib. bdg.)
1. Shakers – Juvenile literature. [1. Shakers.] I. Randolph, Sallie G.
2. Title
BX9771.B65 1990
289'.8 – dc20   89-70618
CIP AC

ACKNOWLEDGEMENTS

The authors are grateful for the opportunity to visit Hancock Shaker Village in Pittsfield, Massachusetts and Canterbury Shaker Village in Canterbury, New Hampshire, two of the special places where the Shaker heritage is being lovingly preserved. Staff members at both villages were knowledgeable and helpful, especially Robert W. Meader, librarian at Hancock Shaker Village; Joan Clemons, former director of public relations at Hancock; and Nancy Thompson of Canterbury Shaker Village.

The authors are also indebted to the thousands of Shaker brothers and sisters who labored so long and so well to create Heaven on earth and whose special genius inspired this book.

*For Christopher Bolick
and Rich Randolph*

CONTENTS

THE SHAKER COMMUNITIES

1 Watervliet, New York
2 Mount Lebanon, New York
3 Hancock, Massachusetts
4 Harvard, Massachusetts
5 Enfield, Connecticut
6 Tyringham, Massachusetts
7 Alfred, Maine
8 Canterbury, New Hampshire
9 Enfield, New Hampshire
10 Sabbathday Lake, Maine
11 Shirley, Massachusetts
12 West Union, Indiana
13 South Union, Kentucky
14 Union Village, Ohio
15 Watervliet, Ohio
16 Pleasant Hill, Kentucky
17 Whitewater, Ohio
18 Groveland, New York
19 North Union, Ohio

Short-Lived Communities
20 Gorham, Maine
21 Savoy, Massachusetts
22 Sodus Bay, New York
23 Narcoossee, Florida
24 White Oak, Georgia

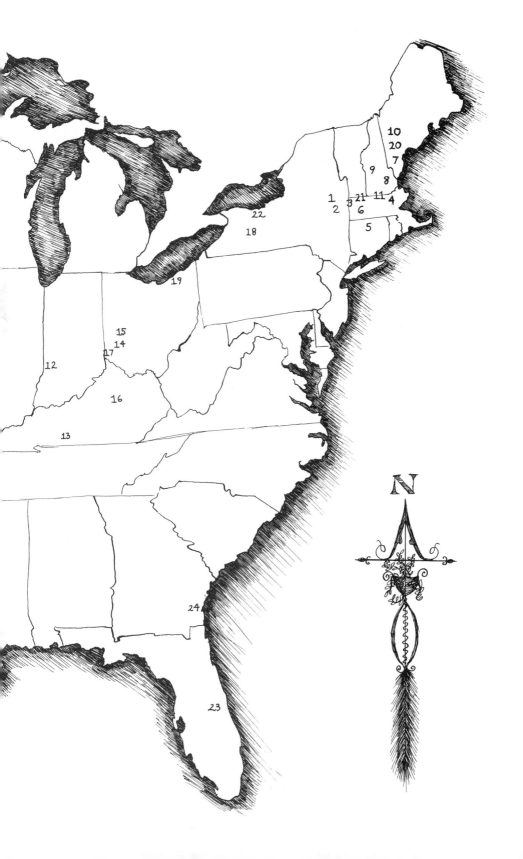

Chapter

1

HANDS TO WORK AND HEARTS TO GOD

"Labor to make the way of God your own.
Let it be your inheritance, your treasure,
your occupation, your daily calling."
Mother Ann Lee

According to a widely-told Shaker story, Sister Tabitha Babbitt, a young woman who was a member of the vibrant Shaker religious community at Harvard, Massachusetts, stopped one hot summer afternoon in 1810 to watch two brethren, or brothers, sawing firewood.

How inefficient the reciprocating saw is, Sister Tabitha thought. It took two men to operate and worked only when it was being drawn straight across the grain.

There must be a more sensible way to cut wood than that, she told herself as she returned to the sisters' workshop to finish her spinning. The spinning wheel whirled while Sister Tabitha thought. Soon she had an idea.

She asked one of the brothers to make her a round metal disk with notches around the outside. She fitted the disk to her spinning wheel so that it would whirl around. Then she tried the spinning blade on a wooden shingle. It sawed through. The brothers refined the design and began to use it in their workshops. Scholarly historical researchers say the Shakers did not invent the very first circular saw, but they were certainly the first Americans to use such tools regularly in the early 1800s.

Sister Tabitha was just a young woman when she devised her version of the circular saw, but she continued throughout the seventy-four years of her life to experiment with ways to make work more efficient and life more comfortable. She watched blacksmiths forge individual nails, pounding each one into shape, and figured out an easier way to cut nails from sheets of iron. She invented an improved spinning wheel and, at the time of her death in 1853, she was working on a way to make false teeth that were less painful to wear and more efficient for chewing food.

Hundreds of important tools, gadgets, machines and labor-saving systems were invented, designed, and

According to an often repeated Shaker story, Sister Tabitha Babbitt got the inspiration for her circular saw while she was spinning wool.

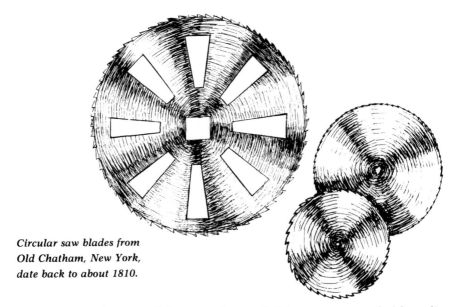

Circular saw blades from
Old Chatham, New York,
date back to about 1810.

improved by members of this same remarkable religious group – the Shakers. Their diverse inventions include the button chair-tilter, Babbitt Metal (a special alloy used in machine bearings), the screw propeller, the sulphur match, and the first commercial washing machine. They built elegant, simple furniture and airy, functional buildings.

"A mania has seemed to take hold of some of the brothers for inventing and being skillful mechanics, and they are successful," a 19th Century Shaker newsletter said. "It is rumored that one of our members is now studying out a plan for a flying machine."

Although it wasn't a Shaker who ultimately invented the airplane, these people were so clever they became well known as remarkable inventors and innovators. In fact, they may have received too much credit for their ingenuity. Modern historians question whether the Shakers actually invented all the things that have been attributed to them. The clothespin, for example, widely believed to be the product of Shaker ingenuity, was actually in use earlier and was credited to the Shakers because of a misinterpretation of old records.

Many Americans, when they saw a useful new product or an intriguing invention, just assumed that it was Shaker-made, although others could have developed similar gadgets and tools. After all, the majority of Americans were farmers in the early 1800s. They did the same kinds of work and used the same types of materials. It would be natural for similar inventions to develop along parallel lines.

Their secret was their sense of community. Because the Shakers worked as a team and not on their own, as small farmers did, when one brother or sister came up with a better tool for doing a job, others were told of it and made copies. Once a device was perfected, the Shakers made many to sell to "the World," so Shaker ideas were indeed likely to spread quickly.

All Shaker children were taught penmanship in school and Shakers usually kept meticulous diaries that described what they believed to be their inventions. Because they kept themselves isolated from "the World," they did not realize that other versions of their inventions had been developed elsewhere.

Shaker villages, where members lived together

in large communal "families," were models of efficiency, prosperity and order. The Shakers were trying to create Heaven on earth by adhering to the three fundamental doctrines of their faith: purity, community and separation.

Purity meant that they did not believe in marriage or physical relations with the opposite sex. It also meant being as free as possible from all types of sin and making their society as flawless as they could.

Community meant sharing. Although the Shakers did not have their own children, they created families of faith. They lived together in special villages, shared everything, owned all their assets jointly, and worked together to provide for everyone.

Separation meant isolating themselves from the

Shakers got their name because of their dancing form of worship. Men and women lined up on opposite sides of the Meeting House and engaged in elaborate ritual dances.

evil influences of society. They dubbed everything that was not Shaker "the World" and tried to be independent of it. Separation also meant that Shakers kept women and men apart from one another, so that they wouldn't be tempted by "sins of the flesh."

Although the sexes were separate, men and women were considered equals who shared leadership and work responsibilities. In fact, the Shaker religion, officially called The United Society of Believers in Christ's Second Appearing, was founded by a woman, Mother Ann Lee, in whose person many Shakers believed Christ had made a second appearance on earth.

Ann Lee was a young woman who belonged to a small, mystical religious sect in Manchester,

England. It may have been influenced by the Quakers, but the members whirled and danced when they worshipped. Mother Ann Lee, as she came to be known, and her fellow believers were often ridiculed

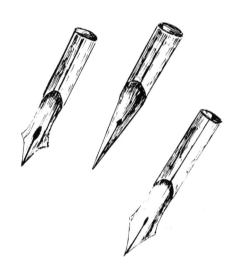

The Shakers were among the first to use metal nibs for pens. The metal nibs, which were dipped in ink before writing, were a major improvement over the quill pens commonly used before.

and nicknamed "Shaking Quakers," or Shakers.

Ann Lee was persecuted for her beliefs and put in prison, where she had visions of starting a new Shaker community in America. In 1774, just before the American Revolution, she led a small band of followers to the New World. The group eventually settled near Albany, New York and, after many difficult struggles, began to create the first Shaker village.

The early years were difficult, but the pioneer Shakers worked hard and gradually attracted converts. They practiced their religion in every aspect of their lives and work, consecrating themselves entirely to a joyful pursuit of perfection. They tried to follow the advice of Mother Ann Lee, who had told them to "do all your work as though it were to last a thousand years and as though you were to die tomorrow."

Eventually nineteen Shaker villages prospered in the United States, from Maine to Kentucky. At their peak, just before the American Civil War, 6,000 Shakers lived in harmony and industry, worshipping God in their own special way and creating a rich legacy of beauty and simplicity.

Chapter

2

NO DIRT
IN HEAVEN

"Clean your rooms well;
for good spirits will not live where there is dirt.
There is no dirt in Heaven."
Mother Ann Lee

Maybe it was because Mother Ann Lee had once worked as a laundress in England that she thought cleanliness was so important. "Be neat and clean," she told her followers, "for no unclean thing can enter Heaven."

To the Shakers, that meant being clean inside and out. They took excellent care of their bodies, they tried to think clean thoughts, and they kept their houses and workshops spotless.

The broom and brush came to symbolize the Shakers' views more than anything else. They swept and scrubbed every inch of their villages. In fact, those

jobs became such an important part of their lives that they created worship dances around them and wrote spiritual songs about sweeping. In the "sweeping gift" and the "scrubbing gift," Shakers joined hymns to sweeping and scrubbing motions to create their own kind of "laboring," or prayer.

Shakers weren't the first to use brooms. People had been tying cornstalks or straw in bunches to make them for a long time. But in 1798, Brother Theodore Bates of the Watervliet colony invented a better model. He discovered that more dirt could be swept faster

Shaker sisters organized laundry in labeled baskets. They heated many irons at once on specially-designed stoves so that hot ones were always available. Wooden forms to dry socks hang from the wall peg.

with bristles bound straight together, rather than in a round bunch. He devised a way to lace the straw into flat brooms and invented a machine to manufacture the improved brooms. After his breakthrough, the Shakers made thousands of flat brooms for themselves and to sell in "the World."

They used Brother Bates's brooms and their

Special racks at the Canterbury laundry dried clothes inside in bad weather. The fires that heated the wash water also produced steam to heat the drying racks.

dusting and cleaning brushes every day. The tidying began before breakfast, when sisters would sweep their rooms and those of the brothers. It ended in the evening, when the brothers cleaned up sawdust and scraps from their workrooms.

All that cleaning brought the Shakers a step closer to Heaven, they believed. But it also took a lot of time and effort. The Shakers valued cleanliness, but they also thought they should have something to show for their hard work. So it wasn't long before they streamlined everything.

Dust and dirt, they realized, collected under furniture and on top of it, on picture frames and tables,

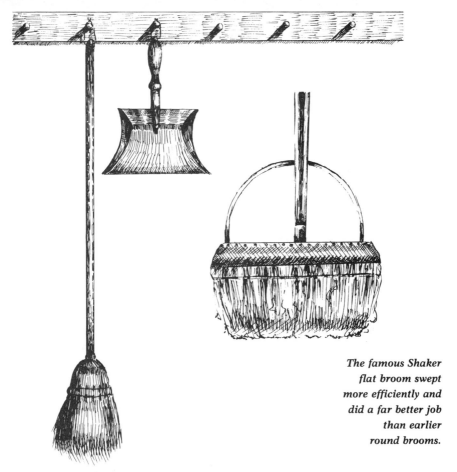

The famous Shaker flat broom swept more efficiently and did a far better job than earlier round brooms.

in corners, and under rugs. Shifting things to get at the dirt seemed like a waste of time and energy. The solution was to keep things simple and easy to move so dust wouldn't mount up.

The Shakers came up with a wonderful idea that solved many problems – wooden pegs fastened in strips onto every wall. The strips were placed about six feet from the floor, the pegs spaced eighteen inches apart. Everything – hats, cloaks, brooms, chairs – was hung on them to make cleaning quick and easy.

The Shakers discovered many other ways to make the work go faster. They put rollers on bed frames to make moving them easy. They screwed wooden slats to window frames and simply loosened the wooden screws when they wanted to tilt the panes in or out to wash them.

They built many desks, cabinets, bureaus and workbenches right into the walls so they didn't have to dust tops and sides. They designed free-standing chairs, tables, desks and shelves with simple lines so as not to collect dust on fancy ornamentation and complicated construction. Today, plain and elegant Shaker furniture is considered beautiful and is highly prized by decorators and antique collectors.

The Shakers kept themselves clean, too. Good health and comfort depended on clean bodies and clean clothes. "Come let us all in love unite, And keep our garments clean and white," admonished one Shaker song.

With hundreds of Shakers living together, getting laundry done was a huge job. Brother David Parker of Canterbury made it easier when he designed a steam powered "wash mill" in 1858. The sisters collected clothes in numbered baskets so they could keep track of whose were whose. They fed the clothes into large vats where they sloshed in boiling water.

The clean clothes were wrung in a mangle, another Shaker invention. It was probably made of Babbitt Steel, a soft metal alloy that didn't heat and reduced friction. Babbitt Steel had been developed jointly by the Shakers and a neighbor, Samuel Babbitt.

Then the clean, wet laundry was pulled up to the second floor in a dumbwaiter, a miniature elevator slung from a pulley. On rainy days the sisters hung the laundry on racks of steam pipes heated by the boiler below. The huge racks fitted into the wall when they weren't in use and slid out on rollers for drying.

Brother Parker's washing machine was so popular that it won a medal at the 1876 Philadelphia Centennial Exposition. Many big hotels ordered copies of it from the Canterbury brothers.

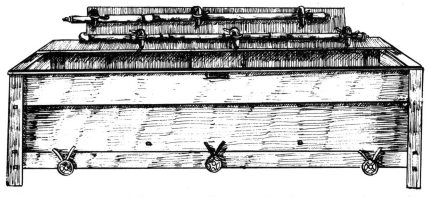

Shakers were the first to build and use large washing machines.
They sold ones like this from Canterbury to many hotels
and commercial laundries.

On good days, the clothes were hung outside to dry, held in place by clothespins. The confusion over the invention of the clothespin probably came from a misreading of Brother Isaac Newton Young's diary. He wrote about seeing a device that turned threads on a pin, which is what a Shaker peg was often called. That differed from a wooden clip to hold clothes on a line. Since George Washington's laundress is supposed to have used small clothespins as well, they couldn't have been invented by the Shakers. But the

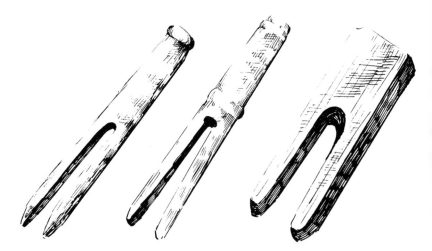

Several styles of Shaker clothespins. It's not certain the Shakers invented them, but they were the first to manufacture them on a wide scale.

Shakers manufactured their own clothespins along the elegant lines so typical of their design.

Clean clothes had to be ironed, and the sisters found efficient ways to do that. At Canterbury Shaker Village in New Hampshire a steam-iron stove heated water that could be sprinkled on clothes to make them softer and easier to iron. Flat irons were placed around the sides of the stove to heat up. An iron stove at Hancock Shaker Village in Massachusetts heated dozens of irons at the same time. Wooden stretchers shaped like feet were used to dry woolen socks and there were arm-shaped wooden boards to iron sleeves on.

In order to save laundering time, the Shakers invented some of the first wash-and-wear fabric back in the 1840's. It didn't wrinkle and it resisted water, too. They did it by laying pieces of linen between

sheets of paper treated with chemicals. Then they heated the fabric in a special screw press until the chemicals had set the linen.

Chapter

3

VICTUALS PREPARED IN GOOD ORDER

"What we deem good order,
We're willing to state –
Eat hearty and decent,
And clear out your plate."
Notice to Visitors in a Shaker Dining Room

The Shakers would shake their heads if they could see the way Americans eat these days. To the brothers and sisters, food was the important fuel that kept them doing God's work. "See that your victuals are prepared in good order and on time," Mother Ann Lee advised the Shaker sisters, "so that when the brethren return from their labors in the fields, they can bless you and eat their food with thankfulness."

The brothers helped to grow and harvest the food, but the sisters did all the cooking. At the height of the Shaker movement, a typical Shaker family might have several hundred members who sat down to eat.

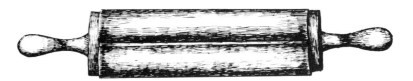

The double rolling pin allowed Shaker sisters to roll out twice as much pastry in half the time.

Shakers also served many meals to visitors.

The way Shakers made one of their favorite foods, apple pie, shows how clever they were. The sisters could produce sixty golden pies in the time it took many American housewives to bake two or three pale inferiors. Their secret: efficient kitchen tools for every job in the process.

First they used the double rolling pin to form twice as much dough in half the ordinary time. They prepared apples with their screw-based peeler that stripped skin off with the turn of a handle. Next, apples were cut into quarters on the spikes of a device designed by Brother Sanford Russell of South Union, Kentucky.

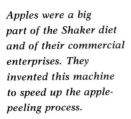

Apples were a big part of the Shaker diet and of their commercial enterprises. They invented this machine to speed up the apple-peeling process.

This woman is enjoying her participation in baking the Shaker's famous apple pies.

Then, sixty pies baked at the same time in the revolving oven Eldress Emeline Hart of Canterbury designed in 1876. As tall as a sister, the oven had four shelves made of pierced iron that rotated and baked the pies evenly. A window made of isinglass, a transparent substance made of gelatin and fish parts, let the baker look inside without losing heat through an open door. The oven did a wonderful job of baking bread and became a standard feature of other Shaker kitchens and bakeries in "the World."

Shakers, like most farmers in the northeast in the early 1800 s, loved apples and found lots of ways to

Once the apples were peeled, they were cored on another original device and assembled into pies. A special revolving oven could bake sixty pies at once.

use them. Their canned applesauce became famous all over the country. They made it by drying apple slices and boiling them in sweet cider until four gallons had simmered down to one. That created a dark, delicious sauce that was incredibly rich and sweet. They put up the apple sauce in specially designed wooden buckets decorated with distinctive Shaker labels. It sold almost as quickly as they could produce it. The things they learned about canning apples made them pioneers in techniques to preserve other foods.

They figured out a way to extract the healing parts of herbs by boiling them in a vacuum pan, ex-

*Cheese press
from Hancock
Shaker Village*

perimentation which led to condensed milk, a by-product of Shaker ingenuity and generosity.

The Shakers had bought a large, ball-shaped vacuum pan to create their famous liquid medicines. In 1853 a widower came to visit his children, who were being raised by the New Lebanon Shakers. His name was Gail Borden, and he was working on ways to make a preserved beef and corn mixture for the army. The Shakers let Borden experiment with their equipment and he successfully made a milk syrup in it. We remember him today through his Borden Milk Company. Modern cooks still use his evaporated and condensed milk. The Shakers later sold a vacuum pan to the Smithsonian Institution.

The Shakers earned a reputation for serving some of the most delicious food available. They were innovative, not only in the tools and gadgets they used to prepare it, but also in the special ways they flavored, cooked and presented it. The secret to their success was simple. They used the freshest and best ingredients available, most of them from their own gardens where no pesticides or chemicals were used. They flavored breads, soups and stews, meats, vegetables, fruits, and cakes with herbs and spices they grew themselves.

Preparing three meals a day for hundreds of

Shakers ate at long tables with place settings in groups of four for efficient serving.

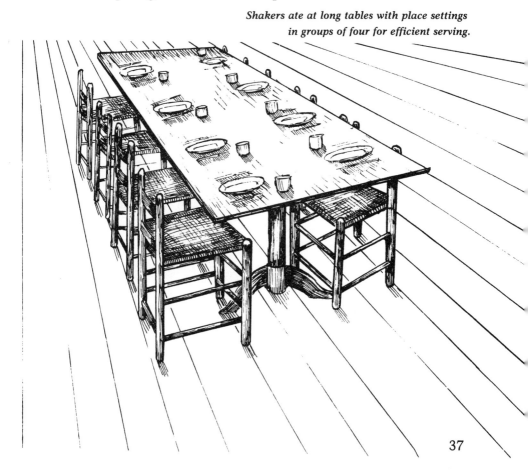

Shakers demanded definite methods and exact measurements. The result was that Shaker cooks pioneered scientific food preparation methods and published one of the first American cookbooks in 1796.

The Shaker sisters looked for quick and efficient ways to make daily food preparation easier and they adapted or invented all kinds of gadgets and kitchen equipment. Many of their devices, such as the slotted spoon, are still staples of modern kitchens. Other food-related inventions include a pea-sheller, a cheese press, a tin box where forty loaves of bread could rise at once, a machine for kneading bread, and one for washing potatoes.

Before each meal, sisters and brothers gathered for fiteen minutes of quiet time before sitting down to eat. At the dining tables they knelt for a silent grace, pulled out their chairs with their right hands, and began to eat in silence as soon as everyone was seated.

The long, spare trestle tables were set simply − no fancy china, tablecloths or centerpieces. Each group of four diners was served its own main dish and condiments. This way no time was wasted in passing food.

In later years, the silence was gently lifted and Shakers talked during meals. Sometimes, in order to save time, one person read the day's newspaper aloud to the group while the diners listened, much like the present-day custom of eating while listening to the news.

The Shaker insistence upon not wasting a thing held true at mealtime, where "Shaker your plate" meant to clean it. In the 1843 *Gospel Monitor,* adults were told not to stuff children with food. "They had much better leave the table hungry, than to eat one mouthful more than is needful." All food left over was used in meals the next day.

Not all apples went into pies. The Shakers were famous for their applesauce, and sold it in distinctively labeled containers.

SHAKER APPLE SAUCE

EAST CANTERBURY

Chapter

4

OH BLESSED, BEAUTIFUL LAND

"Only the simple labors and manners
Of a farming people,
Can hold a community together."
From the Journal of a Shaker Brother

The United States was mainly a farming country in the mid-1800s, when the Shakers were at their peak. Most people earned their living from the land in some way; the Shakers did too.

They did more, however, than just raise animals and cultivate crops. Lovingly tending the land, breeding the best stock, and using every bit of what nature produced was a part of the Shaker religious philosophy.

Many of the people who joined the Shakers were farmers whose families already respected the land. Their goal was to take it from "rugged barrenness

41

into smiling fertility and beauty." The development of the New Lebanon community in New York state is typical of other Shaker villages.

When the community first began in 1789, the brothers planted basic crops — wheat, corn and potatoes. People and animals could survive on these staples and they could be stored for a long time.

Next they laid out a kitchen garden for vegetables, an herb garden, a botanical garden for medicines, and a seed garden. Later came apple, pear, cherry and peach orchards, and fields of strawberries, raspberries and other fruits.

At the beginning, the brothers raised food only for the Shaker family, but as their crops grew larger, they sold what they didn't need to "the World." Their produce quickly earned a reputation for excellence and commanded a good price.

Farms today are run on the power of huge trac-

tors, automatic planters and mechanical irrigation systems. The Shakers started with simple hoes and plows and their own strong backs. But the brothers, always looking for ways to make work go faster and produce better results, soon invented machines to do some of the labor. They designed their own threshing machine. They fashioned a special plow that worked on hills. They built a hay rake and Brother Hewitt Chandler of Sabbathday Lake, Maine, patented the Maine Mower, which made the job of mowing hay fields faster and more efficient. Brother Daniel Baird of North Union, Ohio, invented a revolving harrow; its teeth, mounted on a frame, broke up the soil for planting. Charles Greaves invented a fertilizing machine and another brother developed the first horse-drawn mowing machine.

Horses and oxen provided a lot of the muscle on Shaker farms and they were treated as valuable

This plow from Hancock was specially adapted to use on hills.

members of the community. "A man of kindness to his beast is kind," said a Shaker saying. "Brutal actions show a brutal mind."

The barns at Shaker villages show just how much the Shakers thought of their beasts of burden. They were kept spotlessly clean and well ventilated. Each animal had plenty of room and good food. Even the honey bees were well treated. Elder Henry Blinn of Canterbury Shaker Village in New Hampshire devised a way to air condition the bee hives with adjustable wind vents. And even pests, such a mice, were treated as humanely as possible. The Shakers devised maze-type traps to catch but not injure mice, which were

then released outside.

The round stone barn at Hancock is a marvel of efficiency that allowed one brother to care for an entire herd of up to fifty-two cows single-handedly. Built on three levels, the barn used gravity as well as its special shape to keep the work manageable and the cows happy.

The round barn was not an original Shaker idea, but the many efficient adaptations the Shakers devised for it made it a symbol of Shaker ingenuity. Hay was unloaded into a central spot at the top level called a haymow. Down below, wooden collars held the cows facing inward as they fed at the central

The round barn that still stands at Hancock, Massachusetts, is a tribute to Shaker ingenuity.

Sheep provided wool from which the sisters spun, wove and knitted.

haymow while the brothers milked. Manure dropped through trap doors into the cellar often falling directly onto wagons ready to take it to the fields to be spread as fertilizer.

The North Union, Ohio, brothers found a way to save hay-pitching time. They harnessed a horse to a set of tongs on a pulley. When the horse walked, the hay was thrown up to the loft of the barn on the tongs. All the brothers had to do was spread it around.

The Shaker philosophy of getting the most from what they had led them to breed their livestock scientifically. They imported special strains of cows and sheep from England to improve their herds.

The Shakers treated the land as gently as they did their animals. At Canterbury, the brothers found a way to control pests, make barren soil fertile, and produce power at the same time. In an awesome engineering job, they dug five ponds out of a mosquito-infested swamp. Water from the first pond flowed into the others by a series of stream channels. The brothers built a tannery, sawmill, machine shop, grist mill, and a mill for grinding herbs on the ponds, all of them powered by the same water. After it had powered the mills, the nutrient-rich water was used to irrigate the fields.

The Shaker orchards and wood lots and fields are quiet now, no longer actively farmed. But the fences that marked their boundaries still stand. That's because the Shakers, unlike their neighbors, built for eternity. They made posts out of huge granite slabs.

Solid granite posts anchor the Shaker fences that still stand today.

They sunk them into the ground and anchored the fence slats to the stone. Granite doesn't rot, and the wooden fences still hold their shape today as a · reminder of the prosperous farms that once flourished under innovative Shaker management.

Chapter

5

HEALTH, PRICELESS HEALTH

"A pearly brow that tells of holy thought;
A ruddy cheek, and eye with sparkling light;
Strong, well knit arms that love to do the right;
Free lungs that heave with pure air day and night,
These make of mortal life a sweet delight."
Shaker Poem

The Shakers would have felt right at home with the modern American passion for good health and physical fitness. But their concern with their bodies ran deeper than just looking and feeling good. When their bodies were in top shape, so were their souls, they believed.

Creating Heaven-on-earth, though, was hard work that required healthy people. "It takes a whole man or a woman to be a Shaker," was one of their popular sayings. So they got at least seven hours of sleep every night, ate healthy food, discouraged smoking, used liquor only as medicine, exercised their

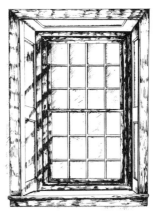

Shaker windows were planned for good ventilation as well as light. The small window panes in this door could be raised or lowered to allow fresh air to circulate.

bodies through hard work, and treated illness with gentle nursing and good medicine.

Doing these things makes good sense today because science has proven how important they are. But in the 1800s, good nutrition and fitness were strange new ideas to people in "the World." In those days, running water, good food and medicine were luxuries that not many enjoyed. The Shaker beliefs in bathing regularly, in keeping fresh air in their homes and workshops, and in producing top quality food, set them apart from the people around them.

Even if their neighbors had shared these Shaker values, it would have been hard for families on small farms to provide them. But the Shakers, living as a community and sharing the work and the rewards, had practical reasons for maintaining healthy habits that prompted them to look for ways to do what hadn't been done before.

For example, people in "the World" didn't take baths very often because it wasn't easy. They had to lug barrels of water into the house from ponds or rivers, and they didn't have bathrooms or kitchen sinks. Bathing in an open tub in the kitchen was neither private nor comfortable.

The Shakers faced the same problems. But because they thought being clean was being holy, figuring out how to get a steady supply of fresh water indoors became part of their worship. That's why they buried wooden pipes in the ground at Canterbury as early as 1797. The pipes carried water from ponds directly to the workshops and dwelling houses, providing plenty of running water for bathing and for washing clothes.

The Shakers believed that fresh air was important to good health, too. "Fresh air is the Shaker

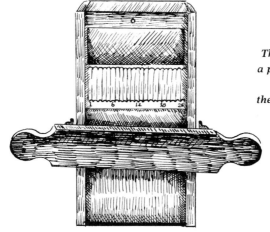

This Shaker invention, a pill-making machine, is now on display at the Fruitlands Museum in Harvard, MA.

medicine," one visitor observed. So they found lots of ways to bring it inside.

Windows, for example, weren't just for looking out or letting in daylight. At Mount Lebanon, many were made so the sashes could move up and down in a way that left an open section in the middle. Fresh air could come in there instead of at the bottom, where it would cause a draft.

Many doors had small window panes that could be lowered to let in air or raised to prevent drafts. Some had transoms at the top that opened and closed for good ventilation. Small holes in the floor beneath steam radiators let in fresh air, and there were even windows built into closets for the same reason.

The Shakers were concerned about getting rid of stale inside air. They designed tin exhaust pipes to carry off gases from candles and oil lamps, and pipe systems that ran from toilets into the chimneys and then outside eliminating bathroom odors. They invented a cast iron chimney cap that could be opened to allow smoke to rise, or adjusted to keep rain and snow out.

Some buildings, like the schoolhouse at Canterbury, had trap doors in the ceiling, worked by a rope

*This handy splint
was adapted
specifically for
broken and
sprained fingers.*

pull, to control the air temperature. In the summer it opened to let the warm air float up and cool the downstairs where the girls studied. The same process in the winter sent the warm air up, so the boys could work comfortably on the second floor.

Of course, the Shakers sometimes hurt themselves at work. And, like everyone else they grew old and died. But, at a time when medicine was still crude, they found ways to nurse each other and make aging a bit easier.

Their infirmaries were as clean as modern hospitals, though without modern equipment. They invented tilting hospital beds, a tin bedpan that could be emptied by pulling out the cork stopper, and a finger splint that slipped over a bandaged finger and kept it in

*Shakers bottled herbs, spices, extracts and
medicines, which were highly approved
and widely used.*

place while it healed. They wrapped a piece of hot soapstone in flannel to create an early heating pad.

And they were famous for the pills, tonics and ointments they made from herbs grown in their gardens. Local Indians taught them the healing value of plants growing wild. Food and Drug Act standards approved many of their preparations at a time when quack remedies were popping up all over.

Wheels turned a typical Shaker chair into an early version of a wheelchair, and gave mobility to invalids who might otherwise be bedridden.

*The Shakers were not always
right. They thought this
static electricity machine
would cure rheumatism.*

Pills were especially popular because they were easier than liquid to store and use. Sure enough, the ingenious Shakers created machines to make the pills. One of them was a flat wooden device with a grooved brass plate on its front. Shaker pharmacists would make a paste of the medicine, then lay it in a strip across the top of the plate. A wooden crosspiece sliced across the gooey paste and divided it into small pieces, which were then dried into pills.

The Shakers were fascinated with new technology, and experimented frequently. One of their less successful but more interesting inventions was a static-electricity treatment machine with which they tried to alleviate the symptoms of rheumatism.

Early Shakers often spent their last days in the infirmary under the care of gentle sisters. Special adult-sized potty chairs and cradles, and even rocking chairs that could be turned into beds, made them feel comfortable and cared for.

Chapter

6

LOVELY GARDEN, LOVELY LIFE

*"Eden was never lovelier.
All nature was praising God
And peace was there."*
Elder Henry Green

Lovely is a perfect word to describe Shaker gardens. They were orderly, fragrant and filled with useful plants of all kinds. Although not planted to be beautiful, they were.

Because they were interested in good health, the Shakers became experts in the use of medicinal herbs. Their appreciation of good food and their wish to be self-sufficient and isolated from "the World" made it important for them to grow vegetables, fruits, herbs and spices in large quantities. They sold their surplus – fresh garden produce, medicinal herbs and packaged garden seeds – in order to purchase the things they could not produce themselves. Their gardens were models of efficiency, worthy reflections of the Heaven on earth they worked to create.

Shaker gardeners planted long rows of rosemary and rhubarb, sage and saffron, peppermint and poppy. Although they did not grow flowers simply for their ornamental beauty, their gardens were filled with brilliant red blooms and heady perfumes.

There were fragrant rows of red roses, whose petals were used to make rosewater. Rosewater had many uses, from bathing patients in the infirmary to adding a subtle sweetness to apple pies. Also from roses came rose hips, which are rich in Vitamin C and are used in medicinal formulas, teas and recipes. When harvesting rose petals, Shaker sisters plucked them apart, leaving the stems behind to avoid the temptation to fasten a fresh rose into their hair or preserve it in water.

Poppies were even more eye-catching, their blowsy red blooms dancing in the breeze. Sister Marcia Bullard wrote about poppies in a 1906 magazine article: "Forty years ago it was contrary to the order which governed our lives to cultivate useless flowers," she said. "Fortunately for those of us who love them, there were many plants which were beautiful as well as useful."

Opposite page: Beautiful gardens were the basis for several Shaker industries. The gardens produced herbs and flowers that were used in medicines and flavorings. Seeds were harvested and sold far and wide.

Sister Marcia remembered extensive beds of poppies which were used to produce medicinal opium. "Early in the morning, before the sun had risen, the white-capped sisters could be seen stooping among the scarlet blossoms to slit those pods from which the petals had just fallen," she wrote. "Again after sundown they came out with little knives to scrape off the dried juice. This crude opium was sold at a large price and its production was one of the most lucrative as well as the most picturesque of our industries."

Growing herbs and packaging garden seeds were two of the most important Shaker industries. The first Shaker herb catalog, published in 1831, offered for sale 154 herbs, barks, roots, seeds and medicinal preparations.

The Shakers became the first in North America to produce herbs for hospitals and for commercial remedies. "The best medicinal gardens in the United States are those established by the communities of the Shakers," said a professor from France in 1851. They "cultivate and collect a great variety of medical plants. They sell them cheap, fresh and genuine." At the peak of the Shaker movement, the medicine gardens at Mount Lebanon covered more than fifty acres and produced hundreds of plant varieties.

Brother Thomas Corbett of Canterbury, New Hampshire, concocted Corbett's Shakers' Compound Syrup of Sarsaparilla "from roots, herbs, and berries grown, selected and discovered by the Shakers." Corbett's Sarsaparilla was distributed wholesale through-

*The Shakers were the first
to package small quantities
of seeds for sale.*

out the late 1800s, and was advertised as "a perfect health restorer for dyspepsia, indigestion, pale, thin and watery blood, malaria and liver complaint, weak nerves, lungs, kidneys and urinary organs, consumption, emaciation and exhaustion of delicate females, nursing mothers, sickly children and the aged." It sold well.

The Enfield, New Hampshire, community made and sold a product developed by Brother Samuel Brown called Brown's Shaker Fluid Extract of English Valerian. The Mount Lebanon Shakers offered the Shaker Asthma Cure, Mother Siegel's Curative Syrup, Shaker Family Pills, and Shaker Hair Restorer, among other medical products.

Because the Shakers had a reputation for honesty and quality, the products of their "physic gardens" were highly regarded. And because they were perceived as mysterious, their mysticism helped sell their products. "By reason of their pure lives, the Shakers, some more than others, are able to read the hearts and minds of men more gross and sensual than themselves," read one advertisement. "This being so, why should they not be able to understand the character of disease and how to cure it better than those who have no insight into nature's mysteries? At all events it is certain that the power of Shaker Extract of Roots, or Siegel's Syrup, to cure where all other remedies are useless, shows the rare knowledge and skill of the people who prepare it."

The Shakers were the first to put seeds in small packages for the home gardener, complete with printed instructions for planting and cultivating. Packaged seeds became one of their biggest businesses.

The industrious Shakers devised tools to help them plant, harvest and sell their products. A rolling spiked wheel poked evenly spaced-holes in the ground. Seeds were released — one at a time — into each hole by a gadget that could be adjusted for different-sized seeds. A single Shaker could operate it with one hand,

A spiked wheel made evenly-spaced holes for planting seeds.

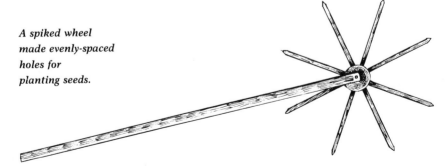

inserting the seed into the soil at the correct depth, stepping over the spot to tamp it down and going on to the next planting, all without having to bend over. With Shaker equipment, planting was done in half the normal time and with no waste of valuable seed.

In order to prepare their herbs for shipping, the Shakers invented a machine that compressed them into dense blocks for convenient handling. They also

Shaker tonics and medicines were thought to have mysterious powers.

designed special chisels to slice through many layers of paper at once, cutting in bulk the right shape for seed packages. And they invented or adapted many gadgets to sort seeds and pills with maximum efficiency.

"The garden is said to be an index of the owner's mind," said a Shaker guide of 1842, *The Gardener's Manual.* If so, it went on, the Shakers must have minds of "order, usefulness and beauty," just like their lovely gardens.

Chapter

7

NO DEBTS
BUT TO GOD

"Hard-headed, shrewd, sensible and practical, [the
Shaker brother] neither cheats, nor means to be cheated,
prefers to give more than the contract demands, glories in
keeping the top, middle and bottom layer equally good in
every basket and barrel of fruit or vegetables sent to
market under his name."
Eldress Anna White

The Shakers did not believe in owing anything
to anyone. They required each new member to clear all
debts before signing the Shaker covenant and entering
a Shaker family. The trustees of each village saw to it
that all bills were promptly paid. Their reputation for
honesty, quality, and good business sense brought
them ready customers. Shaker industries and products
enjoyed steady sales and brought in handsome profits.

When the Shakers built things for themselves
they often devised machines or methods to make them
in quantity to sell. As a result, their workshops were
filled with ingenious machines and tools to sell.

There were double calipers which could measure two dimensions at once. There were machines that split lengths of wood into splints to be woven into baskets. There were machines that turned out large numbers of uniform, smooth staves to make barrels. There were special looms designed to weave the narrow tapes used in their distinctive chair seats.

Although Shaker standards demanded the finest in craftsmanship, the workers were always looking for ways to streamline production and save precious time. Some products were made from standardized parts in a methodical fashion that foreshadowed the modern assembly line.

The Shakers knew the importance of worker satisfaction and rotated jobs regularly, refusing to hurry their work. The pace was steady, not rushed or frantic. "Haste make waste," was one of their sayings.

The Shakers rested periodically from their labor, knowing the value of a break or change of pace.

Oval boxes were a Shaker trademark. Distinctive flexible 'finger' joints allowed the boxes to keep their shape.

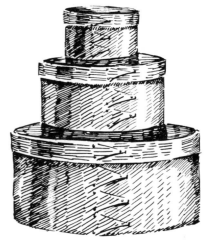

Ash baskets were made to last. They were used to carry many things from apples to laundry, and were highly prized by buyers from 'the World.'

In the laundry room at Canterbury is a special cupboard where cups and plates were kept for refreshments. The sisters there may have pioneered the modern coffee-break.

Among the most popular Shaker-made items were the famous nesting oval boxes which were manufactured with special tools until the last Brother, Delmar Wilson, died in Maine in 1961. Brother Wilson was personally responsible for the construction of thousands of such boxes during his lifetime.

All of the Shaker villages made chairs for their own use and extras to sell, but the brothers created a virtual chair factory at Mount Lebanon, where they constructed the famous ladderback chairs in seven precise sizes. One variation was the tilt-back chair which, because of an unusual device called a boot, enabled the sitter to tilt back without tipping over the chair or marring the floor. The boot was actually a wooden ball with one side carved into a flat plate. It fitted into a socket on the chair leg and was held in place with a piece of leather. The ball rotated in the socket to let the chair tilt smoothly and safely.

Although Shakers dressed plainly, some of their industries catered to fashion in the outside world. Kentucky Shakers experimented with growing mulberries and raising silkworms. They spun silk into fine fabric and made their own handkerchiefs, scarves and ties to sell.

Fine straw bonnets were manufactured in some communities, the work made easier by a variety of machines and molds designed so the preparation of the straw and the shaping of the hats was as simple a process as possible. Many communities made the famous Shaker sweaters, pullovers and cardigans with a distinctive loose knit. Copies are still popular today.

The biggest-selling Shaker fashion was the

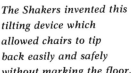

The Shakers invented this tilting device which allowed chairs to tip back easily and safely without marking the floor.

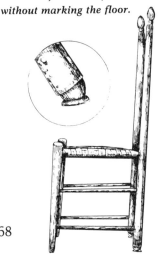

famous Dorothy Cloak, named after an original cape fashioned by Eldress Dorothy Durgin of Canterbury. Sisters in nearly all communities cut and sewed these flowing capes from fine fabric in order to meet a heavy demand for them. President Grover Cleveland's wife wore one to her husband's inaugural ball in 1893.

During the early days of their industries, Shaker brethren loaded carts with brooms and tools, furniture and seeds, and peddled them on long selling

Different shapes and sizes showed how Shakers combined comfort and utility in chairs. Although chairs were manufactured at almost all Shaker villages, the chair factory at Mount Lebanon was world famous.

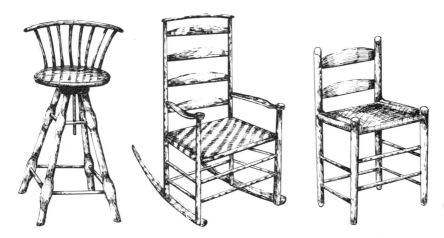

*The "Dorothy
Cloak" was so
fashionable
in 'the World'
that President
Grover Cleveland's
wife wore
one to his
inauguration.*

70

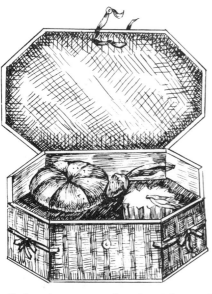

Shaker sisters wove otherwise useless poplar wood
to make sewing baskets to sell. They made
other useful sewing items to sell as well.

Even beeswax went to good use after
the honey was collected. The sisters
at Canterbury made these beeswax
cakes to keep sewing needles rust-
free and to strengthen thread.

Handwrought
iron tailor's
shears were
brisk sellers.

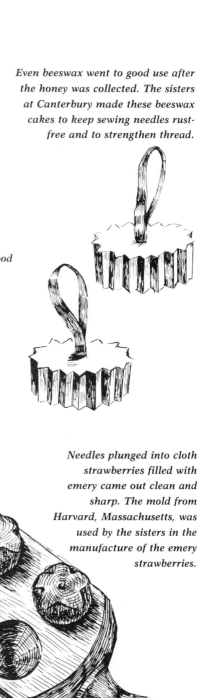

Needles plunged into cloth
strawberries filled with
emery came out clean and
sharp. The mold from
Harvard, Massachusetts, was
used by the sisters in the
manufacture of the emery
strawberries.

A sewing desk built for sister Adeline Patterson (1884-1968) has room for everything she needed for sewing.

trips. As their reputation spread and their sales increased, they adopted other sales techniques.

They offered some products through catalogs by mail. They sold others from shops and showrooms in their villages. In some cases they engaged agents from "the World" to handle distribution of their products. Kentucky brothers took their seeds aboard flatboats and traveled along rivers as far south as New Orleans.

Later, when the numbers of brothers had dwindled, the sisters sold their preserves, fashions, and crafts at fairs and farmers' markets. Even today, a few remaining Shaker sisters keep a shop at their village in Sabbathday Lake, Maine, where visitors can still buy products of Shaker industry and ingenuity.

Chapter

8

A PLACE FOR EVERYTHING

"A place for everything,
And everything in its place."
Shaker Saying

If someone asked a Canterbury sister where to find a particular pair of shears, she might say, "Go into the laundry building and look in the third drawer of the second cupboard on the left of the first room at the top of the stairs." How did she know? Because the Shakers were masters of organization. Order was a fundamental principle that grew from their quest for heavenly perfection.

The sister knew where to find the shears because each building was identified with a letter and each room within it with a number. The drawers and closets and pegs in each room were generally labeled, some with signs and others by charts. Items were often tagged with the code that showed their storage location, and charts were kept for the Shakers to consult should they forget the right place for a particular tool.

The ingenious Shaker wall pegs lined every room for chairs and clothing. Tools and cleaning equipment were also stored on pegs. And such moveable articles as clocks, shelves, candle stands, and sconces were also designed to be hung so that they could be easily relocated as necessity dictated.

All furniture was well made and functional. Whole walls were covered with built-in cupboards and drawers. Drawers were designed to accommodate the item to be stored with never too many things consigned to a single drawer. The Shakers were so neat, they didn't need junk drawers and they didn't let clutter accumulate.

Shaker chests often had drawers on two or three sides, designed to make access easier. Some chairs incorporated a small storage drawer under the seat. Sewing tables were built to accommodate two sisters at work with fold-out cutting surfaces, drawers on several sides, pegs for spools, and specialized nooks for supplies.

Shaker furniture always had a specific purpose. A six-seater school desk at New Lebanon is a good example of such functional design. Three students sat on benches along each side of the desk. Each student's workspace had a flip-over writing panel that covered a storage area with built-in holders for ink and pens.

Inside a Shaker meeting house

The Shakers stored supplies for cleaning in each room, so that it wasn't necessary to sweep across a threshold or carry equipment from one room to another. Their zone method of organization is copied by today's efficiency experts.

When they had a job to do, Shakers often built a special building for the purpose and kept all necessary tools and supplies close at hand. Buildings were conveniently located, and those no longer in use were either torn down and their materials recycled, or were adapted for another use. The thrifty Shakers weren't interested in paying taxes on vacant buildings or wasting time on unnecessary maintenance.

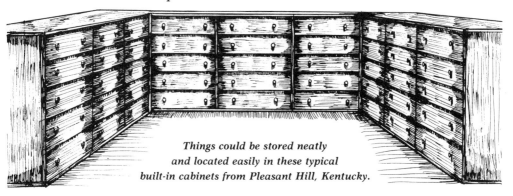

*Things could be stored neatly
and located easily in these typical
built-in cabinets from Pleasant Hill, Kentucky.*

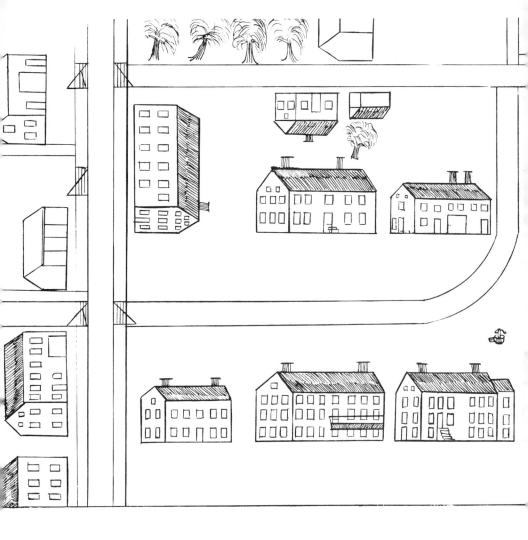

The Shakers were quick to see the usefulness of the automobile and were among the early owners of cars. As soon as they acquired autos at Hancock they needed a place to keep them, so they designed and constructed a sound brick garage, probably one of the first, complete with a system of steam pipes to keep the engines warm enough to start easily. Ironically, that pioneer garage was the last building ever to be built entirely by Shakers.

Shaker villages were carefully laid out for effi-

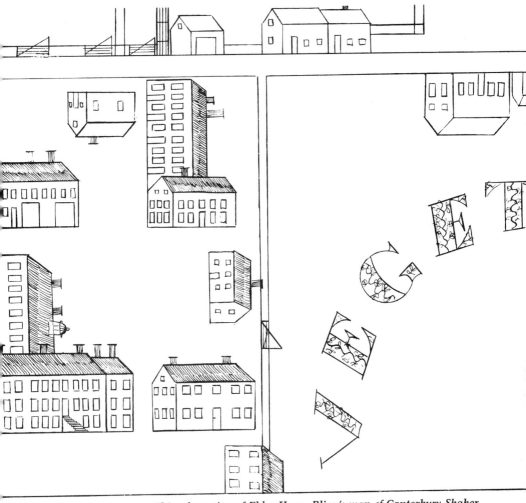

This adaptation of Elder Henry Blinn's map of Canterbury Shaker Village shows the precise placement of pathways and buildings.

ciency and order, designed to reflect what they believed. The straight streets, the plain buildings, and the the fertile fields and orchards were as neat and spare as picturebook drawings. White clapboard meeting houses, dwelling houses – those closest to the road painted brown, those farther back painted red or darker brown – workshops and barns created ordered patterns. Gardens were planted in neat rows and fields were organized to get the most yield for each crop with a minimum of labor and effort. Buildings were used for specific purposes and located for maximum efficiency.

Just as there was a place to work and a place to eat and a place to sleep, there was a place reserved for worship. The meeting house was the most important building and was used only for worship. Here brothers and sisters could free themselves from worldly concerns and concentrate on their relationship with God.

Despite the importance of the meeting houses, the Shakers did not consider them sacred. Worship itself was a sacred activity, but buildings were not. So, when a new meeting house was built, the Shakers had no qualms about adapting the old one to other uses.

The very first meeting house the Shakers ever built, for example, was constructed at Mount Lebanon in 1785 and was the site of early worship and the development of the distinctive Shaker ritual dances. It held a special place in the hearts of the people who worshipped there. But when the Shakers completed a new, larger meeting house in 1824, they converted the beloved old one into a storehouse for the garden seed industry, which had expanded and needed additional places for supplies and inventory. After all, it wouldn't do to waste a perfectly good building when there was another activity to fit the place.

Chapter

9

WASTE NOT, WANT NOT

*"You must not waste one moment of time,
for you have none to spare."*
Mother Ann Lee

The Shakers were not highly educated nor especially brilliant people. They did not have more or better raw materials, or access to technology that was any different from that of their neighbors. Yet they soared high above those around them in the variety of things they produced, their methods of manufacturing, and in the quality of the things they made. Why?

Their basic beliefs drove them to be creative. Do a job as quickly and as well as you can. Use everything and waste nothing. Those simple guidelines, combined with the practical challenge of keeping a large community of people fed and fit, inspired them

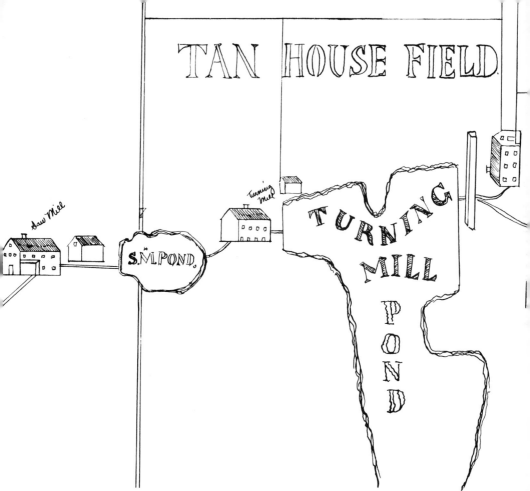

to find new ways to avoid waste.

You can see their philosophy in what two sisters once wrote: The brother, they said "aims to employ his whole being and all his time in the service to which he has devoted himself, yet he sees no virtue nor economy in hard labor when a consecrated brain can work out an easier method."

So the Shakers worked to find ways to use their time, their resources and their materials as efficiently as possible. Their motto was "waste not, want not."

They organized time carefully. Sunday was a day of worship and rest, but every other day started at

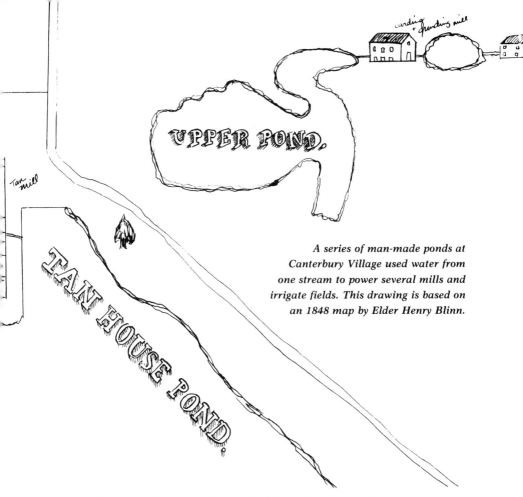

Tan mill

UPPER POND.

carding & grinding mill

TAN HOUSE POND

A series of man-made ponds at Canterbury Village used water from one stream to power several mills and irrigate fields. This drawing is based on an 1848 map by Elder Henry Blinn.

dawn with a few hours of household and barn work before breakfast. Then came time in the workshops until the midday meal, which the Shakers called dinner. With full stomachs, they went back to their chores until supper. The evenings were taken up with more work and a meeting or worship service before everyone went to bed at about nine o'clock.

The Shaker quest for efficiency led to wonderful ideas like the round barn at Hancock, and to the system of ponds at Canterbury. Why use water only once when it could power five different operations? No wonder neighboring farmers said the water was all worn out when the Shakers got through with it.

Even farm animals got into the "waste not, want not" spirit. In the dairies, pigs ate the whey left over from milk and cheese production, and they trailed after the cows and gobbled up the food the cows passed up.

In a Shaker village, corn disappeared without a trace. The animals were fed kernels, the husks were used to stuff mattresses, and the cobs were burned for fuel or to smoke meat.

One of the most striking examples of Shaker efficiency are the boxes that they made from poplar wood. Poplar grew all over the northeast, but it wasn't good for building or burning. Other farmers left it alone, but Brother Granville Merrill created a power machine to shave the "useless" poplar into supple strips. The thin strips were woven on special looms designed by other Shakers. Then the woven wood was backed with paper and formed into over twenty different kinds of boxes and baskets. Woven wood jewelry boxes and sewing boxes were favored best-sellers to "the World."

The Shaker zest for creating ways to save time, energy and materials without cutting corners led to all kinds of small inventions. There were cans with air-spouts that regulated the flow of liquid, preventing even a drip of waste. There were kindling baskets with wooden runners that kept them off the ground and let the air circulate around the kindling, keeping it dry and preventing rot.

Round brushes were devised for dusting corners. Double spools held twice as much thread and didn't have to be changed so often. Paint cans had lids with brushes attached so the paint dribbled inside the can, not down the outside. When the work was done for the day, the top clamped down, holding the brushes in the paint and saving cleaning time and waste. The can-cover-brush also made the painting of ceilings neater and more efficient because the cover caught the drips and recycled them back into the can.

The Shakers also found efficient ways to stay comfortable. They didn't use traditional fireplaces to heat their buildings because most of the heat was wasted — it escaped right up the chimney. Instead they designed wood-burning stoves and used fuel from their villages — logs from the forests and wood scraps from the workshops.

Pipe from a wood stove stretched across the ceiling to spread heat evenly throughout the room.

The Shakers put their stoves in the middle of the room so the heat could radiate out to all sides. Sometimes, as you can still see at the Canterbury schoolhouse, they made double stovepipes that ran across the ceiling and acted as radiators, keeping students comfortable as they did their lessons.

For hot weather, the brothers at Canterbury invented a fan powered by water pumped into the dwellings by their own piping system. The fan had a spigot attached to one pipe so thirsty Shakers could draw a glass of cool water.

There was no room for adornment or art just for beauty's sake, in the world of the Shakers, at least not until the late 1800s when there were fewer Shakers and standards began to lag. But music was an important part of Shaker worship. In the early days, Shakers invented their own shorthand method of writing down music, called letteral notation. Later Brother Isaac Newton Young of New Lebanon made it faster and easier to write down music by designing a pen with a five-point nib. He probably made the nib from melted down silver dollars. When it was dipped in ink and pulled across a page, it drew a complete staff for notes to be penciled in.

A Shaker brother invented the monochord, which couldn't play chords or accompaniments, but could set the pitch at worship. A model of this one-string, violin/piano affair is at Old Chatham. It had tin keys, like a piano, and a short neck. Its single wire was sawed with a bow to make a tone.

People often confuse the Shakers with another religious group, the Amish. But they're quite different. The Amish, who still flourish in the Pennsylvania Dutch country, won't have anything to do with modern life. They still get around by horse and buggy and refuse to use machines or electricity on their farms.

Not the Shakers. If their communities were still thriving, they'd probably love microwave ovens and food processors and all the other time-and-labor-saving devices used today. Extra time for twentieth century people often means more opportunity to play, watch television, or take vacations. To the Shakers, it meant more time to spend in the pursuit of perfection.

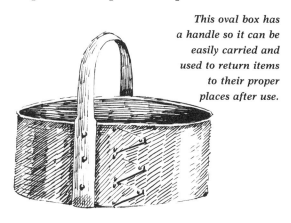

This oval box has a handle so it can be easily carried and used to return items to their proper places after use.

Chapter

10

'TIS A GIFT
TO BE SIMPLE

"'Tis the gift to be simple
'Tis the gift to be free
'Tis the gift to come down
Where we ought to be
Shaker Hymn

Simple is perhaps the best word to describe the inventive Shakers. Sometimes the word simple can mean backward or innocent or crude or dumb, but those certainly are not adjectives that describe the Shakers. They were simple people, but their simplicity was honest and intelligent, elegant and dignified, efficient and ingenious.

The search for simplicity and perfection led the Shakers to a style of architecture that was new and dramatic because it was so basic and unadorned. The meeting house at Enfield, New Hampshire, for example, had a rainbow-shaped roof that rose in an arc over the worshippers, like heaven. The ceiling was painted blue, like the sky.

In other buildings, the Shakers carved soaring staircases with plain, elegant banisters. Often the curving parts of the banisters were crafted from a single piece of wood. In every airy room walls were whitewashed, floors were of bare wood, and trim and beams were stained or painted yellow. Light was let in through large windows with canted openings to maximize reflection. Interior shafts functioned as light wells, funneling light into windows on inside walls.

The Shakers made their own paint and it was excellent. Their special formula lasted so long that paint companies tried for years to copy it. The original paint job, well over a hundred years old, still endures in the Canterbury meeetinghouse.

Reducing everyday needs to the bare minimum was always in the minds of the Shakers. So was the pursuit of excellence and perfection. Items of Shaker design were always supremely functional and well-made. They were simple, but unintentionally elegant in their simplicity.

Shaker furniture was crafted from fine woods such as bird's eye maple, cherry or tiger maple. All the surfaces were smoothed to a simple high gloss. The lines were lean and spare. The result is that the Shakers' functional furniture is considered unusually beautiful by connoisseurs of today – so attractive that Shaker items bring thousands of dollars at auctions.

Their trademark ladderback chairs, with

The design of this candlestand is typical Shaker — big enough to hold a candle, simple enough to prevent dust from accumulating, and devoid of unnecessary ornament.

woven seats and gently curved lower slats for comfort, are good examples of how craftsmen put their beliefs into their work. The quality of the Shaker chairs was so obvious that they were honored for their "strength, sprightliness, and modest beauty," at the Philadelphia Centennial Exhibition in 1876.

Although the shape wasn't original, the Shaker legacy lives on in their distinctive round and oval wooden boxes as well as their carriers, wooden baskets with handles. The sides of the elegant boxes and carriers were joined by fingers of maple that expanded and contracted with the weather. Oval boxes made more than 150 years ago still keep their simple shape and their tops fit as snugly as they day they were constructed.

The Shakers would undoubtedly be proud that their handiwork has survived so well. But they would probably be sad that modern collectors don't value the religious principles behind the simple, beautiful Shaker creations or the values that motivated their many inventions and innovations.

The handicrafts, inventions and buildings of the remarkable Shakers live on, but there are just a handful of Shakers alive now, all of them elderly women at Canterbury and Sabbathday Lake. They are curators of a lost way of life.

Over the past three American centuries, there have been many groups of people who experimented with communal living. Some of them were bound by religious ideals, others by intellectual ideas. The excitement of being part of a group would keep them going for a while, but then the emotional commitment would go stale and the communities would fade.

The Shakers were by far the most successful of these communities, thriving for more than a century and enduring for a century more. But gradually the fire went out for them, too. As the nineteenth century lumbered on, the industrial revolution changed the agrarian character of American society. Manufacturers built mills and factories that produced many of the goods Shakers had once made, and produced them more cheaply. The Shakers just couldn't compete in this modern world.

Along with the industrial revolution came a growing interest in science and a slackening of interest in religion. In the 1860s, after the Civil War, people weren't as attracted to the quiet ways of the Shaker villages as they once had been. The Shakers had more work to do, with fewer members to do it. Eventually they had to pay hired hands to help. The hands were Protestants and Catholics who weren't interested in becoming Shakers.

Brothers always entered the left side of buildings, sisters on the right. This meeting house at Mount Levanon was famous for its distinctively Shaker rainbow roof.

The Shakers had hoped to grow by converting more and more believers to their communities. They had taken in orphans and raised the children of their converts. But the new age brought with it new cities, and the freedom and excitement of the bustling urban centers lured many young Shakers.

The appeal of falling in love and having a family was a natural one that never really went away. Because they didn't marry and have their own children, and because other institutions began providing the care for orphans that had once been available only through the Shakers, their numbers diminished. They weren't able to replace aging believers with young ones. Gradually, the busy Shaker Villages became ghost towns. One after another they closed and consolidated.

So Shakerism has passed away, but its spirit lives on. No other communal group has had as much impact on American culture as the Shakers and no group has ever equaled their astonishing inventiveness. Individually, Shakers were not much different from everyone else. But by pooling their resources and living their religion as a group, they accomplished incredible things.

That would not have surprised Mother Ann. Back in 1774, when she came to America, she predicted her sect would shrink to just a few and reach the point where there wouldn't be enough Shakers to bury their dead. But she also said the Shakers would flourish again someday.

Here at the end of the twentieth century,

Mother Ann's prediction is coming true. The Shakers are few in number, but the Shaker spirit is flourishing, though in a different way. Many of the villages are busy again, living museums filled with visitors eager to learn how these inventive people once lived.

Interest in Shakers has never been higher. Visitors come to Shaker villages in vast numbers to see how the Shakers worshipped, walk through the buildings and marvel at the hundreds of items these gentle people adapted, invented and perfected.

The Shakers may not come back to the crowded and complicated world of today, but the pure and simple Shaker way of life preserved in their villages and in their legacy of inventions still lives. The long reach of the simple Shakers still influences modern life.

INDEX